1,000 YEARS AGO ON
PLANET EARTH

SNEED B. COLLARD III

ILLUSTRATED BY JONATHAN HUNT

HOUGHTON MIFFLIN COMPANY
BOSTON 1999

For Eric Dawson,
my friend and brother through the twentieth century and beyond.
With love,
S.B.C.

For Sabrina and Steven and everything your futures hold.
Love, Uncle Jon
J.H.

The text of this book is set in Adobe Stone Informal.
The illustrations are ink and watercolor on paper.

Library of Congress Cataloging-in-Publication Data

Collard, Sneed B.
1,000 years ago on planet Earth / Sneed B. Collard III ;
illustrated by Jonathan Hunt.
p.   cm.
Summary: Describes events and cultural developments all over the
world 1,000 years ago, including the Americas, Europe, Africa, and Asia.
ISBN 0-395-90866-3
1. Middle Ages—History—Juvenile literature. 2. Civilization, Medieval—Juvenile literature.
[1. Middle Ages—History. 2. Civilization, Medieval.] I. Hunt, Jonathan, 1966–   ill.
II. Title.   III. Title: One thousand years ago on planet Earth.
D117.C654   1999
909'.1—dc21   98-43243 CIP AC

Manufactured in the United States of America
WOZ 10 9 8 7 6 5 4 3 2 1

1,000 YEARS AGO ON
PLANET EARTH . . .

◉ About 250 million people lived on Earth.

◉ Forests covered between 45 and 60 percent of the Earth's land surface.

◉ Only about half of the world's civilizations possessed written language.

◉ Slavery existed in many parts of Asia, Europe, Africa, and the Americas.

◉ People burned wood for light and heat.

◉ Wars for land, power, wealth, and revenge were common.

◉ People traveled by foot, by boat, and on the backs of animals.

◉ Every continent except Antarctica had already been settled.

1,000 YEARS AGO IN
NORTH AMERICA . . .

At least one million Native Americans lived between the Arctic Circle and the tip of Florida. They belonged to more than 500 tribes and spoke at least 300 different languages.

In the western part of the continent, Chaco Canyon became an economic center for the Ancestral Pueblo people, or "Anasazi" Indians. The Anasazi were master farmers, engineers, and architects. They survived in their harsh desert homes by building dams and canals to capture precious rainwater. This enabled them to grow corn, beans, and cotton. The Anasazi constructed more than 400 miles of roads and traded finely crafted pottery and turquoise jewelry with people as far away as Mexico. As their civilization prospered, they began building the Great Houses of Chaco.

To build just one of the Great Houses, the Anasazi cut and laid more than 50 *million* pieces of sandstone. Without the help of animals or wagons, they carried over 25,000 trees from as far as 50 miles away. Once completed, the Great Houses served as important gathering places. Here the Anasazi traded, shared news and, in round rooms called *kivas,* performed ceremonies that renewed their ties with each other and the earth. Meanwhile . . .

1,000 YEARS AGO IN
EASTERN
NORTH AMERICA . . .

Another great civilization prospered—the Mississippian tradition. The greatest Mississippian city was Cahokia, located near the modern-day city of St. Louis. Home to as many as 30,000 people, Cahokia thrived between A.D. 900 and 1400. The Cahokians survived by growing maize, squash, and beans in the rich bottomlands along the rivers. Cahokia also became the center of a vast trading network which imported shells, copper, and many other goods from as far away as Michigan, Florida, and Wyoming.

Archaeologists call the Mississippian peoples the Temple Mound Builders because of the immense earthen mounds they constructed. Using only baskets and wooden and stone tools, the people of Cahokia built more than 120 mounds. They buried important people in some mounds and built temples and meeting places on top of others.

Cahokia's largest mound, Monk's Mound, rose almost 100 feet high and covered 14 acres—the size of a modern shopping center. It towered over a large plaza which held markets and fields for playing *chunkey*, a popular game that involved throwing spears or markers at a rolling stone disk. Large mounds such as Monk's Mound probably had important religious significance for Mississippian peoples and helped establish the authority of their rulers over the rest of society.

1,000 YEARS AGO IN
CENTRAL AMERICA . . .

Mayan people began building the city of Chichén Itzá. A deeply religious people, the Mayans worshiped gods who controlled the rain, sun, harvests, and life and death. To these gods, Mayan rulers often sacrificed their own blood. They pulled rows of thorns through their tongues and pierced their bodies with sharp objects. To keep the gods content, Mayans also sacrificed gold, jade, animals, and other human beings.

The Mayans believed that their destinies were closely tied to time, the planets, and the stars. They kept track of time with accurate calendars that included a 365-day year like our own. In developing these calendars, Mayans became skilled mathematicians. They invented an advanced numbering system that allowed them to predict eclipses, track the movements of planets, and calculate important dates hundreds of years into the past and future.

Their knowledge of math and engineering also allowed the Mayans to build Chichén Itzá's massive stone pyramids, observatories, ball courts, and burial tombs. The Mayans adorned these structures with beautiful murals and hieroglyphs. Mayan hieroglyphs are the only written language to arise anywhere in ancient America. They describe wars, rulers, and important dates in Mayan history.

1,000 YEARS AGO IN
SOUTH AMERICA . . .

Cities and chiefdoms dotted the continent from the high mountains of the Andes to the rich riverbottoms of the Amazon. In the western valleys of Peru, people lived in many independent settlements. By A.D. 1000, however, the Chimu people of the northern coast began conquering these separate settlements, creating an empire the size of Italy.

In their desert capital of Chan Chan, the Chimu built the largest adobe city in history. Ten compounds, or *ciudadelas,* dominated Chan Chan. Each ciudadela covered an area of seven or eight modern city blocks and served as a home for noble families. The Chimu survived in the desert by importing food, water, and other supplies from surrounding areas. They also brought in thousands of craftspeople and laborers from all over their empire.

The Chimu ruled with a strict hand. Criminals were stoned to death and left to be eaten by birds. When a ruler died, his servants were sometimes buried alive with him. But Chimu technology and culture blossomed. Potters and weavers made elaborate ceramics and cotton clothing. Metalworkers molded gold, copper, silver, and bronze into jewelry, religious ornaments, tools, and weapons—the finest anywhere in the Americas.

1,000 YEARS AGO IN
CENTRAL AND SOUTHERN EUROPE . . .

Culture and civilization were floundering. Since the collapse of the Roman Empire in the sixth century, formal education and strong central government had disappeared from most of Europe. The vast majority of people, including the ruling classes, couldn't read or write, and advances in science, medicine, and literature had ground to a halt.

A feudal system of government now dominated Europe. In this system, power was held by nobles, church leaders, and other landowners who owned farms or estates called *fiefs*. On each fief lived craftspeople, servants, farmers, and other subjects. From these subjects, the ruling class demanded labor and taxes. In return, rulers were expected to protect their subjects and not throw them off a fief without good reason.

Some kings tried to piece together larger empires. With the help of the Catholic Church in Rome, Otto the Great and his successors struggled to control large parts of what are today Germany, France, and Italy. Eventually though, local rulers tore these empires apart as they fought to keep power for themselves.

The weak condition of central and southern Europe left the region ripe for attack from outside forces. From the east, Slavic peoples invaded. Muslims from Arabia conquered Spain and fought for control of southern Italy. But the most frightening invasions came from the north . . .

1,000 YEARS AGO IN
NORTHERN EUROPE . . .

The Vikings attacked! The Scandinavian people known as Vikings originally came from Denmark, Sweden, and Norway, where they had lived as farmers, fishermen, and hunters. Between the years 800 and 1050, however, they burst from their homelands in search of new lands, adventure, and wealth.

In sleek, fast ships, the Vikings made lightning raids on defenseless towns and villages across Europe and western Asia. Vikings slaughtered their enemies, ransomed rulers, and seized slaves, silver, and other valuables. They looted and left many places, but they settled in others, taking over parts of Ireland, Scotland, France, and England.

Vikings were intrepid explorers. Swedish Vikings known as *Rus* established the first Russian state and traded with the Christian and Muslim powers of eastern Europe and western Asia. Sailing westward, Norwegian Vikings settled Iceland. In about the year 985, they also became the first Europeans to reach North America—500 years before the arrival of Christopher Columbus.

Viking gods included Thor, the god of storms, and Frey, the god of fertility. Around the year 1000, however, Viking rulers in Russia and Sweden converted to Christianity. Most other Vikings followed suit. Within several decades, the wars stopped and Scandinavians who had settled abroad blended into local cultures.

1,000 YEARS AGO IN
ENGLAND . . .

People struggled to cope with one another and with Viking invaders, just as they did in other parts of Europe. As in central Europe, English society was organized along feudal lines. No central government existed, and different rulers often waged war over land and wealth. In the late 870s, however, Alfred the Great united the southern region of Wessex and became the first true king of England.

King Alfred drove the Vikings from the south and managed to keep them at bay through warfare and payments of silver and gold. He built the first fortified, planned English towns and created an efficient army and navy to defend England. But Alfred's vision extended further than simple survival. He worked hard to restore literacy to England, writing and translating many books himself and requiring government officials and priests to learn how to read and write.

After Alfred died, other kings strengthened England's legal, religious, and government institutions. Between 924 and 939, King Athelstan ordered the first standard currency and coinage to be used since Roman times. This helped the crown control England's large economy. English kings also organized land into shires, or counties—an efficient system of local administration which survives to this day.

1,000 YEARS AGO IN
THE MIDDLE EAST AND MEDITERRANEAN REGION . . .

Islamic culture blossomed. Since the seventh century, the Muslims (members of the Islamic religion) had been expanding their influence. Skilled horsemen, they rode out from their original homelands in Arabia, sacking foreign cities for their wealth, and taking control of local governments. While Muslims allowed Jews and Christians to keep practicing their own faiths, many other people were only given the choice: convert to Islam or die.

By A.D. 1000, the Muslims had conquered a vast empire stretching from Spain to western India. Muslim scholars took advantage of this contact with other cultures. Building on the work of scholars from India, Muslim mathematicians gave us the Arabic numbering system and used it to make great advances in algebra, geometry, trigonometry, and even astronomy. Working from early Greek texts, Muslims wrote medical books that were still being used by Europeans 600 years later.

Spectacular Muslim houses of worship, called mosques, often served as places of learning where people studied law and philosophy. At a time when intellectual activity had almost disappeared from central Europe, Muslim scholars ensured that important knowledge would be passed to later Western civilizations.

1,000 YEARS AGO IN
SOUTHERN AFRICA . . .

A new kind of society was forming. Long before Muslims raced across North Africa, waves of Bantu people had begun spreading from West Africa toward the east and south. As early as the fourth century A.D., some of these people settled on the fertile high plains south of the Zambezi River.

These early settlers were the ancestors of the modern-day Shona people. In what is now the nation of Zimbabwe, they grew grains such as sorghum and millet, but their real wealth lay in cattle. Cattle provided meat and milk and were exchanged to negotiate contracts, cement political alliances, and arrange marriages. In the original Bantu society, most people held equal status, but as the cattle culture developed, the society began separating into different classes based on wealth and power.

By A.D. 1000, the Shona were building cities. On hills overlooking these cities, the elite classes constructed massive stone complexes called *zimbabwes*. Zimbabwes resembled fortresses but were built to symbolize wealth and power. From their zimbabwes, rulers not only ran the cattle business but controlled a profitable trade with the coast. There, Arab merchants brought goods from the Middle East and India and traded them for African ivory, gold, copper, and slaves.

1,000 YEARS AGO IN
INDIA . . .

The Muslims had gained control of much of western and northern India. Meanwhile, in the south, the Chola Dynasty was conquering neighboring kingdoms and using its powerful navy to spread to the east.

Since 2400 B.C., India had been the home of a series of advanced civilizations. These civilizations built large, well-planned cities and produced some of the world's finest artists and scholars. Two great world religions, Hinduism and Buddhism, arose here. These religions focused on self-knowledge and achieving personal enlightenment.

Under the Chola Dynasty, from A.D. 900 to 1200, Indian culture continued to prosper. The Cholas controlled the rich sea trade with China, and their wealth allowed them to build magnificent Hindu temples, such as the one at Thanjavur, which rose 190 feet high. Chola craftspeople adorned these temples with hundreds of finely carved statues of Hindu gods.

Chola temples became important economic and cultural centers. They employed thousands of artists, priests, dancers, and laborers. Many colleges and hospitals were built for the education and care of the people. While Chola fleets spread Indian art, architecture, religion, and government throughout Southeast Asia, the temples helped create a thriving, prosperous society at home.

1,000 YEARS AGO IN
CHINA . . .

The Song Dynasty struggled for power. Like India, China was home to some of the world's oldest, most advanced civilizations. As early as 2000 B.C. the first Chinese states formed, and afterward a succession of rulers grappled for control.

Compared to other Chinese dynasties, the Song Dynasty was weak militarily. Mongolian and Tibetan states constantly threatened it from the north. Nonetheless, the Song Dynasty made a host of important advances, especially in government.

Song government was based on the ideas of the philosophers Confucius and Mencius. They believed that rulers earned the right to govern by leading moral lives and making just decisions. Under the Song, a person could obtain a government job based on his abilities and education—not just through his family or personal connections.

To govern more efficiently, the Song became the first civilization on earth to take advantage of the printed book. The Chinese had invented both printing and paper before the Song, but the Song were the first to use printed books on a large scale. In the year 1000, China was home to 60 million people—one quarter of the world's population. Printed books enabled the Song to educate large numbers of students to govern China's enormous population.

1,000 YEARS AGO IN
AUSTRALIA . . .

About 500 tribes of Aborigines hunted and gathered food throughout the continent. The Aborigines first arrived in Australia more than 50,000 years ago, most likely traveling on boats from Southeast Asia.

Australia provided an abundance of food. Each tribe survived by learning about every plant, animal, and water hole in its territory. Aborigines did not farm, and they owned few possessions. They traveled through their territories gathering or making what they needed as they went.

Like many other ancient peoples, Aborigines regularly set fire to large parts of the countryside. Burning promoted the growth of new plants, which attracted kangaroos and other game. At times, violence erupted between tribes, but this was usually over personal matters. Tribes rarely, if ever, attacked each other to take lands or possessions.

Aboriginal beliefs varied from tribe to tribe. Most believed that in the past, Ancestral Beings, sometimes called "Dreamings," released humans on the earth and breathed life into them and the land. Rainbow Serpents are some of the most important Ancestral Beings. They are linked to creation, fertility, and sometimes great destruction. Aborigines believed that the activities of Rainbow Serpents and other Ancestral Beings created the plants, animals, rocks, and places of Australia.

TODAY,
1,000 YEARS LATER . . .

❧ Human population has grown from 250 million people to six billion people and now increases by almost 100 million people each year.

❧ People have cut down or burned about half the forests that existed 1,000 years ago.

❧ All civilizations possess written language, and most people can read and write.

❧ Most countries of the world have outlawed slavery, but in some countries, people—especially children—are still sold illegally and are often forced to work under other harsh conditions.

❧ People still burn wood for light and heat. We also get energy from hydroelectric, nuclear, and solar power, and by burning coal, gas, and oil.

❧ Wars for land, power, wealth, and revenge are still common.

❧ People still travel by foot, boat, and on the backs of animals. We also ride on bicycles, cars, trains, and airplanes.

❧ People still live in most of the same places we did 1,000 years ago. As the new millennium begins, we are also taking the first steps toward colonizing a new frontier—outer space. Sixteen countries are cooperating to build the first international space station. By the year 2004, this new "star" will be orbiting high above the planet we all share.

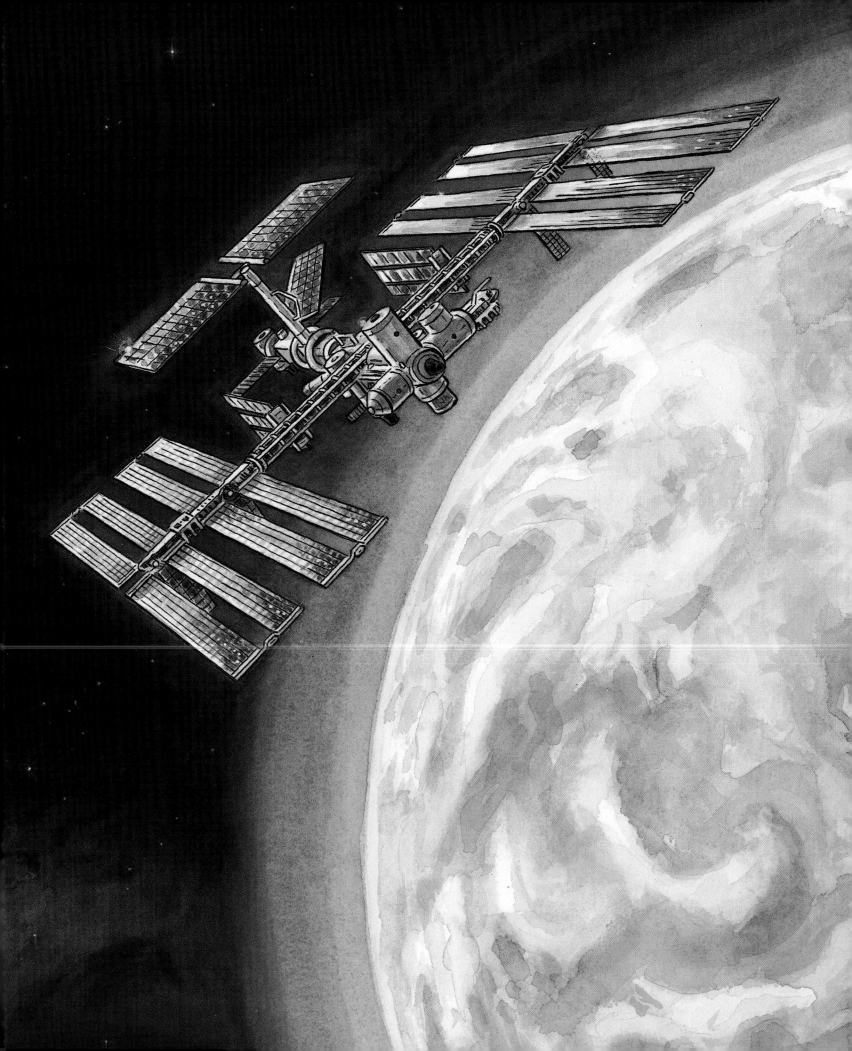

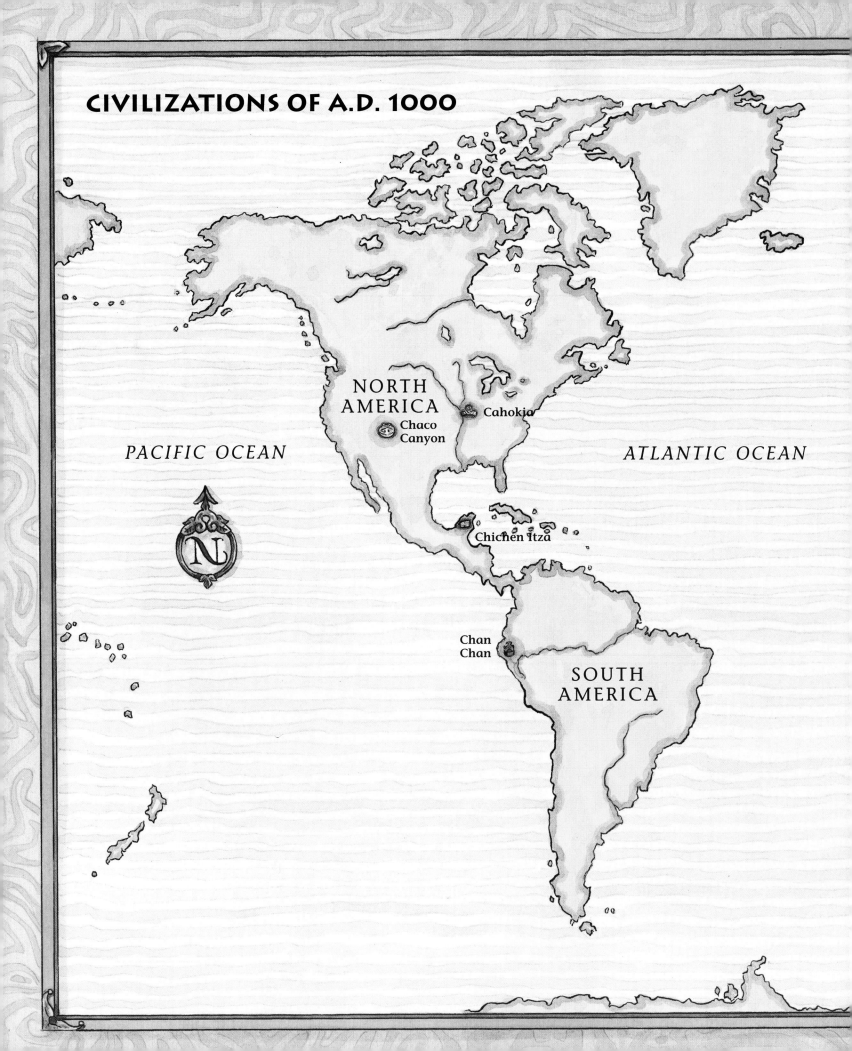

CIVILIZATIONS OF A.D. 1000

PACIFIC OCEAN

ATLANTIC OCEAN

NORTH
AMERICA

Chaco
Canyon

Cahokia

Chichen Itza

Chan
Chan

SOUTH
AMERICA

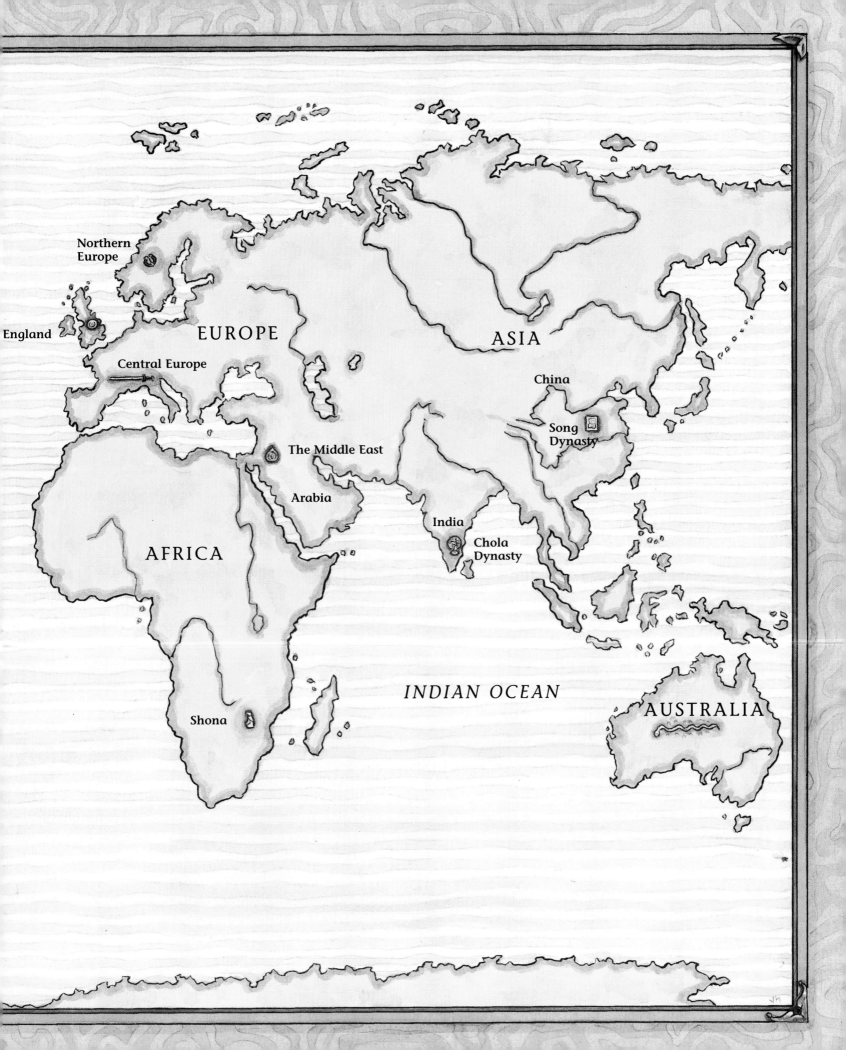

Northern
Europe

England

EUROPE

Central Europe

ASIA

China

Song
Dynasty

The Middle East

Arabia

AFRICA

India

Chola
Dynasty

INDIAN OCEAN

AUSTRALIA

Shona

TO LEARN MORE

BOOKS

Many books have been written about particular ancient civilizations, but few look at ancient civilizations as a whole. Two highly readable and well-illustrated books that do are:

Old World Civilizations: The Rise of Cities and States, published for the American Museum of Natural History by HarperCollins, 1994.

Wonders of the Ancient World, published by the National Geographic Society, 1994.

Two books for young people that may also catch your interest are:

Finding the Lost Cities: Archaeology and Ancient Civilizations by Rebecca Stefoff, Oxford University Press, 1997.

Oxford First Ancient History by Roy Burrell, Oxford University Press, 1997.

WEB RESOURCES

For those with Internet access, many Web sites can be found on ancient civilizations. Two excellent sites that provide links to other "ancient" sites are:

www.n-polk.k12.ia.us/Pages/Departments/media/ancient.html
This site is compiled by the North Polk Media Center in Alleman, Iowa, and is a great way to locate sites about many of the cultures featured in this book.

www.cln.org/themes/ancient.html
This site is sponsored by Community Learning Network, part of British Columbia's Open School program, and also provides links to dozens of sites about ancient civilizations.

Also, the PBS television program *Nova* often produces episodes about ancient cultures and provides excellent, entertaining on-line coverage through its Web site: www.pbs.org/wgbh/nova

Finally, for news about the International Space Station, check out NASA's website: station.nasa.gov/